The Splendor of Birds

An Emma Rose Sparrow Book

Publish Date: November 14, 2015

Editor-in-Chief: Connor Chagnon
Sterling Elle Publishing
Bradford, Massachusetts

ISBN-13: 978-1519317766
ISBN-10: 151931776X

Photo Credits

The artist/source credits for the photos in this book are listed in the order in which they appear:

Cover: Ondrej Prosicky/Shutterstock
Panu Ruangjan/Shutterstock
Steven Blandin/Shutterstock
aaltair/Shutterstock
StevenRussellSmithPhotos/Shutterstock
ArnoldW/Shutterstock
Vitaly Ilyasov/Shutterstock
Edwin Butter/Shutterstock
Colin Edwards Wildside/Shutterstock
Jearu/Shutterstock
assoonas/Shutterstock
Erwin Niemand/Shutterstock
David Byron Keener/Shutterstock
Lovely Bird/Shutterstock
Panu Ruangjan/Shutterstock
Lovely Bird/Shutterstock
JMx Images/Shutterstock
Dan Solomon/Shutterstock
AndChisPhoto/Shutterstock
zahorec/Shutterstock
Birdiegal/Shutterstock
StevenRussellSmithPhotos/Shutterstock
MiQ/Shutterstock
Butterfly Hunter/Shutterstock
Daniel Zuppinger/Shutterstock
Txanbelin/Shutterstock

Colin Edwards Wildside/Shutterstock
Butterfly Hunter/Shutterstock
Nicholas Rexrode/Shutterstock
Ververidis Vasilis/Shutterstock
Neil Walker/Shutterstock
geertweggen/Shutterstock
Stacey Ann Alberts/Shutterstock
Agustin Esmoris/Shutterstock
Kostyuk Alexander/Shutterstock
CW Kuo/Shutterstock
Budimir Jevtic/Shutterstock
Wang LiQiang/Shutterstock
nitat/Shutterstock
karlstury/Shutterstock
shunfa Teh/Shutterstock
Soru Epotok/Shutterstock
Ondrej Prosicky/Shutterstock
Svetlana Foote/Shutterstock
Zoltan Gabor/Shutterstock
Atiwich Kaewchum/Shutterstock

Made in the USA
San Bernardino, CA
13 December 2017